Sadie Spider strikes again

The spider's song

I'm a spider,
    big and scarey.
I'm a spider,
    big and hairy.
Come and sit down
    here with me,
And one of us
    will have some tea.

The fly's song

Spider, spider on
    the wall,
I'm not scared of
    you at all.
Try to catch me
    if you can,
Hairy, scarey
    spider man!

Pat Edwards

That's Sid. He's Sadie's brother.